Little Pebble™

Community Helpers at the Construction Site

by Mari Schuh

CAPSTONE PRESS
a capstone imprint

Little Pebble is published by Capstone Press,
1710 Roe Crest Drive, North Mankato, Minnesota 56003
www.capstonepub.com

Library of Congress Cataloging-in-Publication Data
Names: Schuh, Mari C., 1975– author.
Title: Community helpers at the construction site / by Mari Schuh.
Description: North Mankato, Minnesota : Little Pebble Books, an imprint of Capstone Press, [2017] | Series: Little pebble. Community helpers on the scene | Audience: Ages 4–8. | Audience: K to grade 3. | Includes bibliographical references and index. Identifiers: LCCN 2016009760|
ISBN 9781515724018 (library binding) | ISBN 9781515724117 (pbk.) |
ISBN 9781515724186 (ebook (pdf))
Subjects: LCSH: Construction workers—Juvenile literature. |
Construction industry—Juvenile literature. Classification: LCC TH159 .S38 2017 |
DDC 690—dc23
LC record available at http://lccn.loc.gov/2016009760

Editorial Credits
Megan Atwood, editor; Juliette Peters, designer;
Pam Mitsakos, media researcher; Tori Abraham, production specialist

Image Credits
Alamy: Nik Taylor, 17; Getty Images: Huntstock_Images, 13, IPGGutenbergUKLtd, 11, Yellow Dog Productions, 5; Shutterstock: Andrey_Popov, 19, bikeriderlondon, cover, Dmitry Kalinovsky, 15, kasahasa, 3, 24, back cover, kurhan, 21, Merch Hub, 9, michaeljung, 7, mihalec, 1

Printed in the United States PO007031

Table of Contents

A New Home

Workers come to a job site.
They will build a home.
Who helps at the site?

At the Job Site

Here is the foreman.

He leads the crew.

Let's go!

A machine operator digs.

He moves the dirt.

A framer makes a wall.

It is tall.

Up it goes!

Look up!

A roofer makes a roof.

It is big.

He uses nails.

A mason lays bricks.

He will add stones too.

Good job!

An electrician puts in wires.
She uses pliers.

A plumber adds pipes.

He uses a wrench.

Many helpers work at a job site. They get the job done.

30'
30'
30'

Glossary

electrician—a worker who puts in and fixes electrical items

foreman—the leader of a group of workers

framer—a worker who nails wood together to make a building's walls

machine operator—a worker who drives a machine

mason—a worker who builds or works with bricks, stones, or cement

plumber—a worker who puts in pipes or repairs pipes

roofer—a worker who builds the roof of a building by adding tiles or shingles

Read More

Deedrick, Tami. *Construction Workers Help.* Our Community Helpers. North Mankato, Minn.: Capstone Press, 2014.

Heos, Bridget. *Let's Meet a Construction Worker.* Community Helpers. Minneapolis: Millbrook Press, 2013.

Jeffries, Joyce. *Meet the Construction Worker.* People Around Town. New York: Gareth Stevens Publishing, 2014.

Internet Sites

FactHound offers a safe, fun way to find Internet sites related to this book. All of the sites on FactHound have been researched by our staff.

Here's all you do:
Visit *www.facthound.com*
Type in this code: 9781515724018

Index